John Train's
MOST
Remarkable Names

Commander Sink, U.S.N.

John Train's
MOST
Remarkable
Names

Being a Compendium of *True Remarkable Names of Real People* and *Even More Remarkable Names*, with an Entirely New Collection, Fully Annotated.

by John Train

Illustrated by Pierre Le-Tan
Foreword by George Plimpton

Clarkson N. Potter, Inc./Publishers/New York
Distributed by Crown Publishers, Inc.

Grateful acknowledgment is made for the use of the
material from the following:

Remarkable Names of Real People
Copyright © 1977 by John Train. Used by permission
of Clarkson N. Potter, Inc.

Even More Remarkable Names
Copyright © 1979 by John Train, Illustrations
copyright © 1979 by Pierre Le-Tan. Used by
permission of Clarkson N. Potter, Inc.

Published by Clarkson N. Potter, Inc., 225 Park
Avenue South, New York, New York 10003 and
simultaneously in Canada by General Publishing
Company Limited.

CLARKSON N. POTTER, POTTER and
colophon are trademarks of Clarkson N. Potter, Inc.

Manufactured in the United States of America

Library of Congress Cataloging-in-Publication Data
Train, John.
    John Train's Most remarkable names.
    Includes index.
    1. Names, Personal—Anecdotes, facetiae, satire,
etc. I. Train, John. Remarkable names of real
people. II. Train, John. Even more remarkable
names. III. Title. IV. Title: Most remarkable names.
CS2309.T715   1985   929.4   85-9558
ISBN 0-517-55097-0
10 9 8 7 6 5 4 3 2 1
First Edition

FOREWORD

I had always assumed that John Train's interest in remarkable names stemmed from our undergraduate days at Harvard. We were both members of the humor magazine, the Harvard Lampoon, *and indeed, in turn, its president. One of the inconveniences of holding that office was that the president was held accountable not only for the contents of the magazine but also for the activities of members inevitably hell-bent on doing mischief.* Épater le bourgeois *was a clarion call! However hard he tried to control things, the president was invariably called in by the college authorities and placed on disciplinary probation. Among other penalties, this meant that his real name could not grace the masthead of the* Lampoon, *placing him in a curious limbo state. The way around this was for the president to make up a false name that would then be substituted, so that his identity—at least to insiders—would be preserved. These adopted or "phunny" names (the* Lampoon *editors traditionally substitute* ph *for* f *in penned communications to each other) were supposed to be clever and often were. Various miscreants went under the names J. Norden Baumzeit, Donovan U. Era, Norman Conquest, Natalie Cladd, Bertha von Nation, Oliver Sudden, Ophelia Legg, Annie Climax, a number*

Goody P. Creep, Undertaker

of Mustafas (as in Mustafa Butt), and Warren Peace*. In particularly raucous years the masthead was often more fun to read than the contents.

Neither John Train nor I can remember which, if any, of these "phunny" names we used to cloak our true identities during our Lampoon years. But no matter! It turns out that it was not the Lampoon, but rather an astonishing sequence of events one winter day in 1949 that provided the actual catalyst for the remarkable name collection.

It began with Train leafing through a copy of the now long-defunct Collier's, where he happened upon a list of what someone considered women's funniest first names. Among these were Blooma, Chlorine, Dewdrop, Dinette, Larceny, Faucette, Twitty, and Zippa. Also mentioned in the article was a resident of the town of Hoquiam, Washington—one Katz Meow. As Train put it to me, "I thought this was all very useful information, which I dutifully noted down in the back of my engagement book."

Later that day Train ran into Howard Mumford Jones of the Harvard English Department. He mentioned his list of women's funniest first names. He also brought

*A real-life Warren Peace turns up in this volume, an ex-Williams student—a classic case of life imitating art. A Mustafa also can be found in the text (collected by John Train), which the reader can find for himself.

up Mr. Meow. Upon which Professor Jones disclosed that he had a secretary during his Army days named Miss Magnetic Love. She, in turn, had a friend who was also in the secretarial pool named Miss Pensive Cocke.

His mind doubtless reeling from the excitement of entering two new names in his Daily Reminder, Train repaired to Cronin's, a favorite student tavern of the times, where his day was capped off by the astonishing revelation of a friend, Richard (Sandy) Gregg, who produced a postcard from an uncle disclosing that his landlady in Tryon, North Carolina, was named Melissy Dalciny Caldony Yankee Pankee Devil-Take-The-Irishman Garrison!

Perhaps not since "the gentleman from Porlock" knocked on Coleridge's door has there been such a day of literary import, except that in one instance (Coleridge's) a major work was halted; in Train's case a most important endeavor commenced: the formation of the Office of Nomenclature Stabilization to help families "on the verge of settling for Dora or Chuck" to do far better with their imaginations.

A word about the authenticity of the names. Many readers simply do not believe that parents can put their heads together and come up with such nomenclative oddities to bestow on their innocent offspring as Immaculate Conception Finkelstein. Such is the probability of skepticism that Train (and the Office) have gone to great pains to verify each entry with solid documentation. Easier to pass through the eye of a needle than to grace these pages!

One such skeptic was a talk-show host who challenged Train by picking a name at random from the collection and, during the show, placing a long-distance telephone call to one Halloween Buggage of New Orleans. Halloween Buggage not only answered the phone but informed the startled and doubtless humbled talk-show host, that it was the practice in the Buggage household to name offspring after the day of their birth, if it happened to be a holiday, and that she indeed had a younger sister in the other room named Easter Buggage. Right there on the show Train's pencil came out and Easter Buggage went into his MM's Daily Reminder. How warming to consider that in the future a Buggage may be born on Labor Day. Or All Saints Day!

I have asked Train if he felt that some of the remarkable names could cause psychic damage to their bearers. Was it possible to go through life with the name Odious Champagne, a paper-mill employee from Winslow, Maine? No to the first, yes to the second. Train felt it was like any other peculiarity—being too tall, or short, or having too pronounced a nose—one not only learned to accept such things, but very often used such idiosyncracies to advantage. "It may be odd," he said, "today not to have an odd name."

The clincher, of course, is that it is possible to change one's name if it causes too much offense or loss of self-esteem, and very few bearers of remarkable names have chosen to do so. A. Przybysz took the opportunity to change his name to C. Przybysz. LeGrunt E. Crapper changed his to LeGrant E. Crapper. Apparently, bestowed with one of these names, it is hard to let go. Theanderblast Mischgedeigle Sump, Train tells me, gets very upset if his middle name is left out of correspondence to him.

I asked: "Have you ever met Sump? I'm talking, of course, of the Mischgedeigle Sump. Or some of the others in your book?"

Oh yes, I was told. Not Sump. But Train had talked on the phone to I. M. Zamost. Father O'Pray had been in his house. Heidi Yum-Yum Gluck (whose name had been offered but ample documentation could not be discovered in time for the first volume) had invited him to her art show. "Fully verifiable. Very modern painter," Train recalled. "Huge rectangle of black with a faint purple line."

"Who else?"

"Welcome Baby Darling, a Connecticut advertiser. I've talked to Dr. and Dr. Doctor, also from Connecticut. In the course of verifying Hyman Peckeroff I not only found him but got into his cab and took a ride. Made my day! Oh, there have been many."

"Have you met I. P. Frilli?" I asked.

"Oh yes."

"Is he all right?"

"Yes, he's all right. A Florentine car mechanic."

I asked what his personal favorites were in the collection.

"I am very fond of Nosmo King—some harried parent being inspired by what he or she saw on a waiting room wall. An 'elegant solution,' as they say in mathematics. Also, I like Mark Clark Van Ark. It's hard to pick one out."

He thought for a while and then came full circle, back to that winter day in 1949.

"It's hard to beat Katz Meow, isn't it?"

Meeting John Train for the first time would not suggest a presence for whom humor has much meaning. His expression is New England dour. A long beak of a nose. The lengthiest expression of mirth I have heard from him is a quick, double-barreled heh-heh, *but more usually a single note,* heh, *the second* heh *cropped off with a giant shears as if to prevent an outburst of uncontrollable mirth.*

That is not to suggest that there is anything crotchety about John. He has been this way as long as I've known him—one of those schoolmates who seemed far beyond his years (in league, perhaps, with the faculty!*) and who has not changed over the years: the eternal* Lampoon *president, full of easy erudition and wit that, fortunately for a vaster audience, are on display in this inestimable volume!*

George Plimpton

Hugh Pugh, Landscape Architect, London

How To Name Your Baby

As most parents know instinctively, there is a curious magic in names. Call your little one Elmer, *and he will be less likely to succeed than if you plunge in with a* Charlemagne *or a* Napoleon. (*Had the Emperor been christened* Gaston *he would surely have remained stuck as an obscure officer of artillery.*)

General Ulysses Grant . . . *what panache! Led by a* Hiram (*the General was in fact christened* Hiram), *the boys in blue would have cracked; President* Oscar Lincoln *could not have held the Union together. There would have been no Bicentennial. And speaking of panache, one knows that if Rostand had not celebrated* Cyrano de Bergerac *but* Paul Blanc *he would have flopped in the provinces and never made it to Paris, let alone to immortality.*

The bizarre confections now chosen by many American families for their infants are not as remote as one might think from the customs of an earlier day. Before the Conquest the inhabitants of an English village would devise a novel first name for each child that came along, like yachts or racehorses, so no family names were needed. Thus, only a handful of English kings before William the Conqueror—or Bishops of London, as one sees from their tablet in St. Paul's—bore the same name as any of their predecessors. After 1066, however, England's new Norman masters required that all given names be drawn from

Mr. Vice, Malefactor, New Orleans

a hagiology of about two hundred recognized saints. Then as now, the choices were not distributed evenly over the whole spectrum, but clustered around a few particularly popular ones, e.g., William. This meant that in all but the smallest hamlets, duplications occurred, so surnames became necessary.

America is heading the other way, toward the elimination of the family, particularly in the younger generation. Today's kids, one gathers, were devised by parthenogenesis, or perhaps in the lab, without paternal intervention. "Dad, this is Jennifer and Nicole." Parent, sotto voce: "Jennifer and Nicole who?" Child: "Huh?"

As the family sinks into anomie, *and family names with it, a broader repertoire of given names will be required for identification. The present volume will, we hope, push out the limits of the possible. Anxious parents can see how others have solved the same problems that they now confront. Look in the Index for the appropriate family name (e.g.,* Reuss, *on page 61) and then find suggestions at the pages indicated.*

Every source cited is in the files and has been verified.

We have a number of "detached" given names which are available for general use, including the following twins: Ivory *and* Larceny *(Chicago); and* A.C. *and* D.C., Bigamy *and* Larceny, Pete *and* Repeat, *all from the Florida Bureau of Vital Statistics. From the same source come* Lavoris, Teflon, *and* Truewillinglaughinglifebuckyboomermanifestdestiny. *Others include* Chlorine, Coita, Dewdrop, Faucette, La Morte, La Urine, Margorilla, Mecca, Merdina, Phalla, Twitty, Uretha *and* Zippa (*girls*), *and* Arson, Blasphemy, Blitzkrieg, Bugger, Cad, Constipation, *and* Overy (*boys*), *all from Mencken;** Dinette *and* Lotowana *are from The Social Register and* Buzz Buzz *and* La Void *from* Farb.† *A recent visitor to Jamaica has authenticated Little Tits.* (Desiré Tits *published a book in Brussels in 1945.*)

Nominations for the next edition—always, please, with documentation—will be gratefully received, and should be addressed to the Office of Nomenclature Stabilization, Box 157, R.D. #2, Bedford, New York 10506.

Most undocumented submissions prove to be inaccurate or nonexistent. My favorite in this category is that of Mrs. Wilson of Hewlett, New York:

> *There was one name I came upon in the Nassau County telephone book. That is the only one I'd care to remember but of course I've forgotten it. It bordered on the pornographic. How any mother latched that first name on that last name, I couldn't imagine. I have no idea what either was.*

**H. L. Mencken*, Supplement II: The American Language. *New York: Alfred A. Knopf, 1948.*

†*Peter Farb*, Word Play. *New York: Alfred A. Knopf, 1974.*

Lotta Crap

I have made the surprising discovery that what one might call the free-form nutty name—Oldmouse Waltz, Cashmere Tango Obedience, Eucalyptus Yoho—*is the one indigenous American art form. (Another contender, the totem pole, is also found in New Guinea, and is extinct in America anyway; jazz, said to have originated in New Orleans funeral processions, derived from existing European and African elements.) Some foreign names, notably English, have a poetic ring, but almost never as a result of fantasy. In an English or Chinese name of the richer sort, logic underlies every element, as in a heraldic device; it's not, as with* Membrane Pickle, Odious Champagne, Fairy Clutter, *and* Lobelia Rugtwit Hildebiddle, *the free music of imagination.*

Take one of my favorites, a timber merchant of Sandusky, Ohio, Mr. Humperdinck Fangboner. *Like a good* Times *crossword, the surprising parts join to produce an extraordinary whole.* Fangboner, *to start. Note the cutting edge, the spearhead:* Fang. *A clear warning— Don't Tread on Me. And the strength of the reinforcing* Bone. *Nothing supine or spineless there. It has the sinister force of Dickens's* Murdstone. *Then consider the sprightly yet harmonious overture:* Humperdinck. *First, the ominous* Hump, *evoking the ship of the desert . . . tracks across the shifting dunes, whining houris, glowering sheiks, petrodollars; or the hump of the hunchback, conferring good fortune on whoever touches it; or indeed the erotic sense of hump: fevered couplings of houris, of*

6

camels, of hunchbacks . . . but enough. Soon comes the sprightly grace note of Dink, in, as it were, allegro spiritoso time, with its refreshing contrast to the somber weight of Hump and Fang—a spoonful of sherbet between two rich plates of a sumptuous banquet.

And then, like the resolution of the primary and secondary themes of a symphony, the full Humperdinck, suggesting musical genius, Hansel and Gretel wandering in a wood . . . so fitting for one called by destiny to deal in the products of the forest. Finally the magnificent consummation, the whole orchestra, tutti, fortissimo, in C major: HUMPERDINCK FANGBONER. A recondita armonia . . . evocative as a verse of Mallarmé, a haiku of Bashò.

I find nothing comparable to these American fantasies in other cultures, except here and there in fiction. Dickens, to be sure, the Mozart of the funny names business, showed a marvelous power of onomastic invention, but it fell to the New World to plant its flag upon the heights to which he pointed the way. America, not old England, brought forth Katz Meow, Positive Wassermann Johnson, and Unable To Fornicate, just as so many of the visions of Jules Verne were finally reduced to practice by the National Aeronautics and Space Administration.

As a by-product of détente the Office of Nomenclature Stabilization is considering a branch in the Soviet Union. After the Revolution, optimistic comrades favored names *like* Tractor *or* Electrification. *One enthusiast called his twin daughters* Anarchy *and* Utopia. *A frequent practice was to contrive such acronyms as* Melor *(Marx-Engels-Lenin-October-Revolution). Now that the Revolution has turned sour and become something they would rather not think about, and with even* Pravda *deploring these "tasteless inventions," the classless parents are at a loss. Authoritative guidance will, we understand, be welcome. We shall be there, obstetrical bag packed, as always, not with forceps and chloroform, but with our trusty microfiches and thesaurus. Our preliminary approved list includes* Peaceful Coexistence *and* Virgin Lands *for girls, and for boys,* Norm, SAM, *and* Posthumous Rehabilitation.

John Train

ACKNOWLEDGMENTS

I am most grateful to the following correspondents not already thanked in previous editions: Susan Berman, Hon. Robert S. Carswell, Mark Dixon, David Fleming, James R. Groves, Henry B. Goldberg, Peter Gumpel, Glen Kilner, Debra Kimble, A. J. Lane, Larry Laneer, Thomas J. Manning, Tony Moss, Judge M. L. Tyrwhitt-Drake, Jerry Ward, and Judge Don J. Young; and particularly to my wife, Francie Train.

The Boring School

A. A. A. D'ARTAGNAN UMSLOPAGAAS
DYNAMITE MACAULAY
   (London *Times*)

AIDA QUATTLEBAUM*
   Westminster, California

ANIL G. SHITOLE†
   Rochester, New York

AL DENTE
   Policeman‡
   Plantation, Florida
   (*The Miami Herald*)

*Compare Tosca Zerk, daughter of Oscar Zerk, inventor of
the Zerk Auto Grease Gun.*

†*Compare Pupo Shytti, Vice-President of Albania, Mrs.
P. Shittachitta, Mililani Town, Honolulu, Hi.* (Honolulu
Star Bulletin), *and Ms. Somchittindepata, Ithaca, N.Y.
Atholl McBean is a San Francisco social leader.*

‡*Resigned, complaining pay inadequate.*

A. Moron
   Commissioner of Education
   Virgin Islands

Anne Aass
   Pittsburgh, Pennsylvania

Appendicitis, Laryngitis, Meningitis,
Peritonitis, and Tonsillitis Jackson
   (*Newsweek*)

Argue & Phibbs
   Solicitors
   Albert Street, Sligo, Ireland

Arizona Zipper
   New York City
   (*Village Voice*)

Arystotle Tottle, a timid pyrate

ARYSTOTLE TOTTLE*
Pirate
Falmouth, England

ASA MINER†
Wakefield, Rhode Island

ATOMIC ZAGNUT ADAMS
Son of Founder of Gesundheit Institute
Arlington, Virginia
(*The Washington Post*)

A. TOXEN WORM
Theatrical Press Agent
New York City

*"*A timid pyrate.*" Gosse*, A History of Piracy. *New York: Tudor Publishing Co., 1934.*

†*Compare Asia, Africa, America, and Europe Hamlin. Another brother, Hannibal, Vice-President of the United States 1861 to 1865, nearly lost the election for Abraham Lincoln because brother Africa Hamlin was widely supposed to be black.*

Aurora Borealis Belsky*
    Staten Island, New York

Ave Maria Klinkenberg
    Yonkers, New York

Private Baby Cherry†
    225th Quartermaster Battalion
    U.S. Army

Badman Trouble‡
    Chief Baggage Handler
    Pan American Airways
    Roberts Field, Liberia

Bambang Winneboso
    Banker
    Bank of America
    Ceylon

*Compare Vernal Equinox Grossnickel, Blanchester, Oh.,
and Aurora Cabangbang, Va. (Division of Vital Records
and Health Statistics, Department of Health, Richmond, Va.).

†Compare Private Parts, U.S. Army, and Private Murder
Smith, British Army.

‡"He was, and gave us a lot of," reports our correspondent.

Aurora Borealis Belsky

BAMBINA BROCCOLI*
    New York City

SIR BASIL SMALLPEICE
    Chairman, Cunard Line
    London, England

BATHSHEBA FINKELSTEIN
    High School of Music & Art (Class of 1957)
    New York City

B. BROOKLYN BRIDGE
    (John Hancock Life Insurance Company)

MRS. BELCHER WACK WACK†

BETTY BURP
    (Bureau of Vital Statistics, Jacksonville,
    Florida)

*Compare Concerto Macaroni.

†Miss Belcher married Mr. Wack twice.

Concerto Macaroni

Rev. Blanco White*

Mr. Boeras†
    Registered Colon Therapist
    Sarasota, Florida

Dr. Bonebrake
    Bonebrake Chiropractic Center
    Wichita, Kansas

Bonnie Bee Buzzard‡
    "The Roost"
    Wayland, Massachusetts

* *A waverer. Ordained a priest in 1800; thereafter Professor of Religion. Renounced Christianity and abandoned the priesthood, 1810. Re-embraced Christianity, 1812; re-ordained, 1814* (Dictionary of National Biography). *Another Blanco White is a Divorce Commissioner in London.*

†*The Compiler has his professional literature.*

‡*Compare Sir Farquhar Buzzard, personal physician of King George IV.*

THE BORING SCHOOL*
   Boring, Oregon

BUFORD PUSSER†
   Heroic Sheriff
   Selmer, Tennessee

BUGLESS, ENERGETIC, EUPHRATES, and
GOLIATH SMITH‡
   (Indexes of Births for England and Wales)

DR. BULL§
   Pennsylvania State Secretary of Agriculture
   Philadelphia, Pennsylvania

*Compare the Cretin School, St. Paul, Minn., and the
(Gov.) Dummer School. Dr. Boring, dentist, drills away in
St. Petersburg, Fla., while the Rev. Boring soothes his flock
in the Bethel Alliance Church in Sandusky, Oh.*

†*A suspicious car crash ended his career in 1977. Compare
Cotys Mouser, chief clerk, U.S. Senate Committee on
Agriculture and Forestry.*

‡*Cited in Dunkling,* First Names First. *London:
J. M. Dent and Sons, 1977.*

§*Subject of celebrated headline:* BULL TO SPEAK ON
ARTIFICIAL INSEMINATION.

19

Messrs. Bull and Schytt
Glaciologists
General Assembly, International Union of
Geodesy and Geophysics
Geneva, Switzerland

Bumpus McPhumpus Angeledes
Virginia
(Division of Vital Records and Health
Statistics, Department of Health,
Richmond, Virginia)

Buncha Love*
(*Newsweek*)

Bunyan Snipes Womble, Lawyer, and
Calder Wellington Womble†
Winston-Salem, North Carolina

*Compare Félicité Pratt Love (known to the Compiler),
Holy Love, and Wonderful Love, all of New York. (Miss)
Magnetic Love was a secretary in the Army Air Corps.
Hastie Love was convicted of rape in Tennessee. For
Vaseline Love et al.* vide infra.

†*"He enjoyed discussing the hyphen which in 1913 forever
linked the towns of Winston and Salem," and for which,
indeed, as head of the Winston Consolidation Committee,
he was in large measure responsible.*

Buncha Love

C. A. Faux-Pas Bidet*
　　Commissaire de Police
　　Paris, France

Rev. Canaan Banana
　　President
　　Zimbabwe

Carbon Petroleum Dubbs†
　　Founder, Universal Oil Products
　　Des Plains, Illinois

Cardiac Arrest da Silva
　　Municipal Tax Collector
　　Brazil
　　(*Financial Times*)

Cardinal Sin
　　Archbishop of Manila
　　Philippines

The Sûreté's ace on Russian intrigues, Faux-Pas Bidet received heavy press coverage in the 1930s when he investigated the abduction of Gen. Kutylpov, a White Russian leader in Paris. The general was seized in the street by OGPU agents and apparently, wrapped up as merchandise, was carried on board a Soviet ship, the Spartak, which immediately put out to sea.

†*Also introduced the Japanese beetle to Bermuda.*

Cardinal Sin, Archbishop of Manila

CARESSE PECOR*
    University of Vermont (Class of 1971)
    Burlington, Vermont

CARLOS RESTREPO RESTREPO RESTREPO
DE RESTREPO
    Medellin, Colombia

CASHMERE TANGO OBEDIENCE†
    Agriculturist
    Santa Cruz, California

*Compare Hadassah Pecker, Physician, New York City.

†Compare Clarence O. Bedient, New York Times ad salesman.

CHIEF C. CROOK*
    Police Chief
    Brunswick, Ohio

CHARITY BALL
    Wichita, Kansas
    (*Wichita Eagle*)

CHARLES EVERYBODYTALKSABOUT, JR.
    Seattle, Washington

CHARLOTTE BLOB
    Director, Unidentified Object Center
    Appleton, Wisconsin
    (*Kansas City Star*)

*A different Chief (B.) Crooke heads the Montgomery
County, Md., police force. Narcissus Frett is Chief
Confidential Investigator, Surrogate Court of Kings
County, N.Y. The publisher of Law and Order, on the
other hand, is Mr. Copp.

Cheatham & Steele, Bankers

CHEATHAM & STEELE*
Bankers
Wallowa County, Oregon

CHERRI PANCAKE†
Curator, Museo Ixchel del Traje Indigena
Guatemala City, Guatemala

REV. CHRISTIAN CHURCH‡
Florence, Italy

*The Compiler has a photograph of this establishment.
Compare Haddah Cheatham Wright, owner, Cheatum's
Style Shoppe, Grand Island, Nebr., and Wylie Cheatem,
Attorney General of Texas. T. Swindella was charged with
fraud in London Bankruptcy Court, and Robyn Banks is a
teller in the First Pennsylvania Bank, Chestnut Hill, Pa.
(The Philadelphia Inquirer).

†Compare Golden Pancake, Marion, Oh., and Breece d'J.
Pancake, author.

‡Worked with the Compiler in 1966 flood relief effort.
Compare Christ Apostle, of New York City, Rev. God, of
Congaree, S.C., Rev. Christ Church, of Spartanburg,
S.C., and the Rev. Hosanna, United Church of Christ,
Denver, Colo.

CHRIST T. SERAPHIM
Judge
Milwaukee, Wisconsin
(*United Press*)

CIGAR STUBBS
(Bureau of Vital Statistics
Jacksonville, Florida)

(MRS.) CISTERN BROTHERS*
Hog Neck, North Carolina

Compare Knighton Day, New York City.

MR. CLAPP*
> Venereal Disease Counselor and Lecturer
> County Health Service
> San Mateo, California

COL. CLARENCE CLAPSADDLE
> U.S. Army (West Point, Class of 1940)

CLAUDE BALL
> Seattle, Washington
> (*Seattle Post-Intelligencer*)

DR. CLAUDE ORGAN
> Surgeon and Director of Boys Town
> Omaha, Nebraska

*"*Kept very busy indeed*" by conditions in the late sixties.*

Sir Cloudsley Shovel, Admiral, Royal Navy

SIR CLOUDSLEY SHOVEL*
Admiral, Royal Navy

*Concluding a distinguished career, he ran the fleet on the rocks (Scilly Isles), drowning 2,000 men. As they steered into danger, a seaman who knew the waters warned of their peril. Sir Cloudsley, enraged, ordered him instantly hanged. When disaster struck, Sir Cloudsley, accompanied by his pet whippet, set off in his admiral's barge, which sank in turn. After struggling ashore, he was done in by a peasant woman who "coveted an emerald ring on one of his fingers, and extinguished his flickering life." He was buried in Westminster Abbey, "where an elaborate monument in very questionable taste was erected to his memory" (Dictionary of National Biography). His gallant successor, Admiral Steel Bellie, recovered the Nicobar Islands; Admiral The Hon. Sir Reginald Aylmer Ranfurley Plunkett-Ernle-Erle-Drax participated in the Battle of Jutland. Captain Strong Boozer commanded the Guantanamo Naval Base, but Royal Navy Shippe has opted for life ashore with the Federal Reserve System, Washington, D.C. For Commander Sink, U.S.N., vide infra.

C. Mathews Dick*
   Social Leader
   Newport, Rhode Island

Mr. Cock married Miss Prick†
   (London *Times, 1963*)

*Compare Dr. Dick, urologist, of Colorado Springs, Colo.,
the Griesedick (beer) family of Minneapolis, Minn., and
D. Biggerdick, Art Instruction School, Minneapolis, Minn.
The Dick Tool Company operates in Bronxville, N.Y.

†Mr. Ora Jones married a Miss Ora Jones in 1941
(R. L. Ripley).

Mr Cock married Miss Prick

Comfort and Satisfy Bottom, Sisters

COMFORT and SATISFY BOTTOM*
    Sisters
    Wayne State University
    Detroit, Michigan

COMMODORE DEWEY THIGPEN
    Janitor
    Corpus Christi, Texas

CONCEPTION DE JESUS
    New York City

CONSTANT AGONY†
    Chazy Lake, New York

*Compare Bump and Twinkle Quick, brother and sister, Silvester, Ga. Also Silas Comfort Swallow, 1904 Prohibition Party candidate for President, Rosey and Dewey Butt, sister and brother, Peru, Ind., and Dreama Bottoms, Duke University, Durham, N.C.

†Compare Agonia Heimerdinger, Santa Ana, Calif.

REV. CORNELIUS WHUR*
Trashy Poet (1782–1853)
England

*An impression of the Rev. Whur's output can perhaps be
conveyed by the following:*

The Female Friend

In this imperfect, gloomy scene
Of complicated ill,
How rarely is a day serene,
The throbbing bosom still!
Will not a beauteous landscape bright
Or music's soothing sound,
Console the heart, afford delight,
And throw sweet peace around?
They may; but never comfort lend
Like an accomplished female friend.

With such a friend the social hour
In sweetest pleasure glides;
There is in female charms a power
Which lastingly abides;
The fragrance of the blushing rose,
Its tints and splendid hue,
Will with the season decompose,
And pass as flitting dew;
On firmer ties his joys depend
Who has a faithful female friend.

CRANBERRY TURKEY BRECKENRIDGE, JR.
Virginia
(Division of Vital Records and Health
Statistics, Department of Health,
Richmond, Virginia)

CRYSTAL TOOT
President, Kansas State PTA
Great Bend, Kansas

C. SHARP MINOR*
Silent Movie Organist
Rochester, New York

*Compare O. Pinkypank, ukelele instructor, Sweet
Springs, Mo.

CUMMING & GOOING
Louisiana
(*The New Yorker*)

CUPID RASH*
England
(*Western Morning News*)

DAPHNE READER'S DIGEST TAIONE
Utui, Vavao, Tonga

DR. DEADMAN†
Pathologist
Ontario, Canada

DEFRED GOO FOLTS
Director of Placement
Harvard Graduate School of Business
Administration
Cambridge, Massachusetts

Father of nine; succeeded in getting eleven years behind in his rent before being evicted from public housing project. Another Cupid Rash lives in Toledo, Oh., (Toledo Blade).

†Compare Mr. Deadman, F.B.I. analyst in trial of murderer of 28 young blacks in Atlanta, Ga.*

Cumming & Gooing, Louisiana

Demetrus Plick, Interior Designer

DEMETRIUS TOODLES
Public School 92M
New York City

DEMETRUS PLICK
Interior Designer
Boston, Massachusetts
(Harvard Medical School *Alumni Bulletin*)

DENNIS ELBOW
Fisherman
Warsaw, New York
(*Orvis News*)

DR. & DR. DOCTOR*
Westport, Connecticut

*Known to the Compiler. (One M.D. married another.)
There were, by recent count, 13 doctors Doctor, Docter, or
Doktor in the U.S.; 5 doctors Bonebreak; 1 Bonecutter; 18
Butchers; several Cutters and Carvers; 184 Paines or Paynes;
and 11 Pangs. Dr. Bonesetter practices in Bombay, India,
and Dr. Screech in Victoria, British Columbia. For Dr.
Ovary, gynecologist, vide infra. Among the Mormons, the
seventh son of a seventh son may be named Doctor. W. Doctor
Dollar, N.Y., has not yet entered the profession, but should.
Dr. Falces (pron. "falsies") performs breast implants at
St. Luke's Hospital, San Francisco, Calif.*

DOOLITTLE & DALLEY
    Estate Agents
    Kidderminster, England

DR. DOTTI*
    Psychiatrist
    Rome, Italy

D. SCHUMUK†
    Political Activist
    Ukraine, U.S.S.R.
    (*Reuters*)

EARLESS ROMERO
    Lafayette, Louisiana
    (Courthouse Records)

ECSTACY GOON
    (Wisconsin Historical Society,
    Madison, Wisconsin)

*Once husband of Audrey Hepburn. Compare Dr. Dement,
psychiatrist, Stanford University, and Jean Wierdo, mental
patient, New Jersey State Hospital at Greystone Park.*

†*A loser. Served 7 years in jail (prewar) for communism.
Then (postwar) served 20 years and in 1972 started an
additional 10 years plus 5 years exile, all for anticommunism.*

D. Schumuk, Political Activist, Ukraine

SIR EDWARD PINE-COFFIN
    Poor Relief Commissioner*
    Dublin, Ireland

EPAPHRODITUS, ONESIPHORUS, and
(ARCHBISHOP) NARCISSUS MARSH
    (*New York Times*)

E. PLURIBUS EUBANKS†
    Longshoreman
    San Francisco, California

EUCALYPTUS YOHO
    Ashland Oil Dealer
    Portsmouth, Ohio

EVAN KEEL
    Goldsboro, North Carolina

EVE I. WARMFLASH
    Clark University, Class of 1980
    Worcester, Massachusetts

During the 1844–45 potato famine.

†*Compare E. Pluribus Gass, Western Reserve University, Cleveland, Oh.*

44

E. Z. MILLION
    Director
    Southwest Computer Conference
    Tulsa, Oklahoma

FAIRY CLUTTER
    Indiana University of Pennsylvania
    Women's Club
    Indiana, Pennsylvania

FAITH POPCORN
    Advertising and Public Relations Executive
    New York City

DR. FANG*
    Dentist
    Tillman Clinic
    Belmont, Massachusetts

*Dr. Gargle, New York City dentist, has now retired to Florida. Dr. Toothaker, a dentist with the Arizona Public Health Service, was killed by a rock fall while visiting the Navajo National Monument. Dr. E. Z. Filler practices dentistry in Roslyn Heights, N.Y., Dr. Pull in St. Cloud, Minn., Dr. Warmflash in Stamford, Conn., Dr. Pulls at St. Mark's Clinic, New York City, and Dr. Screech in Essex, England.

Fauntleroy Schnauz

FANNY HUNNYBUN*
    Nanny
    South Devon, England

FARTINA GREENE†
        Virginia
        (Division of Vital Records and Health
        Statistics, Department of Health,
        Richmond, Virginia)

FAUNTLEROY SCHNAUZ
        (Educational Testing Service,
        Princeton, New Jersey)

DR. FEALEY‡
        Gynecologist
        West Palm Beach, Florida

*Met and married Mr. Hunnybun, guest of employer. Died in 1975, aged 97. Compare Fanny Finger, New York City.

†Compare Sharon Willfahrt and Tunis Wind, both of the Art Instruction School, Minneapolis, Minn.

‡Compare Dr. Paternite, Obstetrician, Akron, Oh., and Dr. Fillerup, Obstetrician, Pasadena, Calif.

FEMALE JONES*
> University of Maryland Hospital
> Baltimore, Maryland

F. G. VERENESENECKOCKKROCKOFF†
> San Francisco, California

FIRMIN A. GRYP‡
> Banker
> Northern California Savings &
> Loan Association
> Palo Alto, California

(MISS) FISHY STEP§
> Pennsylvania

*This not unusual given name—bestowed by hospitals in the absence of a parental decision—is often pronounced fe-mà-le. Compare Legitimate Jones and Male Infant Kilgore, both of Detroit, Mich.

†Defendant in a celebrated murder trial in 1897. See Jennings, Personalities of Language. London: Gollancz, 1967.

‡Compare Mr. Overcash, President, American Credit Corporation, Dallas, Tex.

§Arrested for vagrancy. Compare Felonious Fish, Omaha, Nebr., Halibut Justa Fish, Mastic, N.Y., and Fish Fish (London News Chronicle).

Felonious Fish

Madame Fouqueau de Pussy, Authoress

FORTUNATE TARTE
    Mary Fletcher Hospital,
    Burlington, Vermont

REV. FOUNTAIN WETMORE RAINWATER*
    Circuit-riding Preacher
    Kentucky

(MADAME) FOUQUEAU DE PUSSY†
    Authoress

BRIGADIER FRIED BURGER
    Commander, Royal Brunei Malay
    Regiment
    Brunei

*Liked to sprint to church, read one verse from the Bible, and sprint home.

†Le Grand-père et ses quatre petits fils. Boston: Hickling, Swan and Brown, 1855. Compare Graze Pussy, New York City, and Grace Marie Antoinette Jeanne d'Arc de Repentigny, maiden name of Grace Metalious, trashy novelist. Robert Baby Buntin Dicebat's collected poems were published by Constable, London, in 1934.

Mrs. Friendly Ley*
Mission Hills, California

Fuzzey Television, Ltd.†
St. Peter Port, Guernsey, Channel Islands

Baroness Gaby von Bagge of Boo
(*New York Times*)

Garnish Lurch‡
Railway Engineer
Jamaica Government Railways
Jamaica

On whose career of amiability the curtain descended when her husband's revolver, which he was cleaning in the kitchen, went off.

†*Establishment patronized by the Compiler.*

‡*At the throttle when a derailment killed 178 excursionists and injured several hundred more* (The Daily Gleaner, *1957, Kingston, Jamaica*).

Mrs Friendly Ley, Mission Hills, California

GEARBOX MPOFU*
>Automobile Mechanic
>Al Dorn Service Station
>Gweru, Zimbabwe

GENGHIS COHEN
>Student
>Orewa, Rodney County, New Zealand

GINGER SCREWS CASANOVA†
>Eureka, California
>(*Eureka Times-Standard*)

GISELLA WERBEZIRK-PIFFL‡
>Actress
>Vienna and Hollywood

Compare Joy Auto Collision, Toronto.

†*Compare Mutual Screw Company, New York City.*

‡*Niece of Archbishop of Vienna and perennial victim of prewar Hollywood jokers who liked to telephone from poolside to ask if she was the Gisella Werbezirk-Piffl they had met in (e.g.) Monte Carlo the previous summer; on receiving assurance to the contrary, they would pronounce grandly, "Ah! Then that must have been* another *Gisella Werbezirk-Piffl!" Compare Josette Legg Snowball (Actress, D'Oyly Carte Company).*

genghis Cohen

GLASSCOCK VERSUS BALLS
    Much-cited mortgage case
    (24Q.B.D. 13, 6T.L.R. 57)

GORILLA HARISON*
    Virginia
    (Division of Vital Records and Health
    Statistics, Department of Health,
    Richmond, Virginia)

GRECIAN T. SNOOZE†
    Australian University Student
    (Class of 1950)

*Female (born 1924).

†Dunkling, op. cit.

GRETEL VON GARLIC
New York City

GROANER DIGGER*
Undertaker
Houston, Texas
(*Today's Health*)

HALLOWEEN and EASTER BUGGAGE
New Orleans, Louisiana

*Compare Goody P. Creep, Undertaker. A Mr. Bones is an
undertaker in Glasgow, Scotland, Will Plant in Mumbles,
Swansea, Wales, and J. Posthumus in Grand Rapids, Mich.
(Playboy). The Quick-Park Funeral Home for many years
reposed at 617 Columbus Avenue, Sandusky, Oh. The Wing
On Funeral Home is found in Toronto, the Mole Funeral
Home in Barnwell, Ga., and Human & Pitt Funeral
Services in Pretoria, South Africa.*

Hannibal Toto*
    Rome, Italy
    (*Daily Mail*)

Hardon Cox†
    Virginia
    (Division of Vital Records and Health
    Statistics, Department of Health,
    Richmond, Virginia)

*At a wedding, was requested to fire a salute; complied,
using a shotgun, wounding the groom and twelve of the
wedding guests. Compare A. "Tony" Toto, pizza maker of
Allentown, Pa., who was shot in the head by his wife and
others, then drugged, and two days later shot again in the
chest. He survived, and furnished bail to release his wife
from prison, saying, "In my opinion it was lack of
communication—a big lack of communication" (Associated
Press).

†Compare Adora Cox, Crapo, Md., and Mrs. Peedee Cox,
Planned Parenthood counselor, Corpus Christi, Tex.

MR. HEADLINE
    News Director, CBS News
    Washington, D.C.

HECTOR SPECTOR*
    Royal Canadian Air Force

HEDDA HARE
    Spring Valley, New York

HEIDI YUM-YUM GLUCK†
    Painter
    New York City

*Compare Hubert Boobert, trombonist, Marion, Oh.

†Known to the Compiler. Mr. Gluck père, infatuated by
Gilbert and Sullivan, named his son Nanka, after Nanki-Poo,
another character from The Mikado.

HEINRICH LXXIV

Prince Heinrich the Seventy-Fourth of Reuss,
Thuringia, Germany

PRINCE HEINRICH THE 74TH OF REUSS*
  Thuringia, Germany
  (*Almanach de Gotha*)

HENRY FORD CARR†
  Central City, Kentucky

HENRY WILL BURST
  (London *Times Literary Supplement*)

HERMAN SHERMAN BERMAN‡
  Commissioner of Deeds
  Bronx, New York

Since 1693 all males in this ancient family have been named Heinrich.

†*Compare Iona Ford and (Mr.) Zeus Garage, industrial designer.*

‡*Compare Wong Bong Fong of Hong Kong* (Philadelphia Inquirer) *and Fang W. Wang, mutual fund executive, New York City.*

HILARIUS FUCHS*
> Continental Grain Company
> New York City

HOGJAW TWADDLE†
> Morris Harvey College
> (now University of Charleston)
> Charleston, West Virginia

HONOR ROLL
> Nurse-anesthetist
> Birmingham, Alabama

*Compare Hilarious Conception, Hawaii. Continental
Grain's subsidiary ContiCommodities, a commodities
brokerage firm, launched three mutual funds for speculating
in commodities. All three lost so much money that they had
to be closed down. ContiCommodities then incurred such
heavy losses and litigation from customers (reputedly between
one and two hundred million dollars) that it was itself
disposed of.

†Has found his name a valuable aid in breaking the ice
with new acquaintances. Compare Sianah E. Twaddle,
San Mateo, Calif.

Hilarius Fuchs, Continental Grain Company

Miss Horsey de Horsey

HORACINE CLUTCH
Pelham, New York

(MISS) HORSEY DE HORSEY
Intimate friend of Lord Cardigan*

HROTHGAR HABAKKUK
Vice-Chancellor, Oxford University

HUGH PUGH
Landscape Architect
London, England

*Who on a notable occasion banged on her door, shouting,
"My dearest, she's dead!"—referring to her late Ladyship—
"Let's get married at once!" Compare the Honorable
Outerbridge Horsey, U.S. Ambassador to Czechoslovakia.

HUMPERDINCK FANGBONER*
    Lumber Dealer, and
    FANNY FANGBONER
    Nurse
    Sandusky, Ohio

HYMEN & COX†
    Opticians
    Cambridge, England

ICCOLO MICCOLO
    Piccolo Player
    San Francisco Symphony

*Folks in Sandusky, as in some towns in Oklahoma, seem to feel better having odd names. Other citizens of the area include Ovid Futch, Xenophon Hassenpflug, Kitty Ditty, and (from the Sandusky Register) E. Kickapoo Banfill, Lecturer.

†Compare Hyman Peckeroff, taxi driver, New York City (known to the Compiler); Hyman Pleasure, Assistant Commissioner, New York Department of Mental Hygiene; and Buster Hymen (San Francisco Examiner).

I. C. SHIVERS*
    Iceman
    (John Hancock Life Insurance Company)

IF-JESUS-CHRIST-HAD-NOT-DIED-FOR-
THEE-THOU-HADST-BEEN-DAMNED
BAREBONES†
    London, England

IGNATZ DANGLE
    Grand Rapids Hospital,
    Grand Rapids, Mich.

ILONA SCHRECK-PUROLA‡
    Skin Pathologist
    (*Club* magazine)

*Compare Bluey Cole Snow, another John Hancock policy-
holder; Norman Icenoggle (Associated Press); E. Horry
Frost, Incorporator, Safeway Stores, Baltimore, Md.; and
(Miss) Icy Hoar, Department of Defense, Washington D.C.*

†*Set up the first fire insurance office in Britain. Changed his
name to Nicholas Barbon. Compare Through Trial And
Tribulation We Come At Last To Heaven Slappe (London
News Chronicle).*

‡*Coauthoress*, Baldness and Its Cure.

Ingeborg von Zitzewitz

IMA HOGG*
> Social Leader
> Houston, Texas

IMMACULATE CONCEPTION FINKELSTEIN†
> New York Stock Exchange Investor

I. M. ZAMOST‡
> Lawyer
> Highland Park, New Jersey

INGEBORG VON ZITZEWITZ§
> New York City

*Ura Hogg is a myth, but Ima June Bugg is a daughter of the Administrator of the Farmington, Mo., State Mental Hospital.

†South American customer of Oppenheimer & Co., New York City. Compare Modest Newcomer Weisenburg, University of California, Berkeley, Calif.

‡Known to the Compiler.

§Known to the Compiler.

IONA VICTORY BOND
    Victoria, British Columbia

I. O. SILVER
    Doctor
    Hazel Crest, Illinois

I. P. FRILLI*
    Master Mechanic
    Florence, Italy

IRIS FAIRCLOTH BLITCH
    Congresswoman
    Washington, D.C.

ISRAEL GESUNDHEIT
    Bankruptcy petitioner
    Seattle, Washington

**Known to the Compiler. Compare P. P. Fast, Fla., and
Tom Passwater, Art Instruction School, Minneapolis, Minn.
A Mr. Uren changed his name to Wren (1897)—
understandably.*

Iva Odor*
    Schoolteacher
    Spencer, Iowa

Sir Jamsetjee Jejeebhoy†

Mr. Jockitch married Miss Grubb‡
    Cuernavaca, Mexico
    (*Park Avenue Social Review*)

*Compare Rev. Ivan Odor, Owosso, Mich.

†"*Son of Rustamjee J. C. Jamsetjee Jejeebhoy and Soonabai Rustomjee Byramjee Jejeebhoy. Succeeded cousin, Sir Jamsetjee Jejeebhoy 6th Bt., and assumed name of Jamsetjee Jejeebhoy in lieu of Maneckjee Rustomjee Jamsetjee Jejeebhoy. Chairman, Sir Jamsetjee Jejeebhoy Charity Funds, Sir Jamsetjee Jejeebhoy Parsee Benevolent Institution; Trustee, Sir Jamsetjee Jejeebhoy School of Arts, Byramjee Jejeebhoy Parsee Benevolent Institution. Heir, Rustom Jejeebhoy*" (Who's Who).

‡*Known to the Compiler. Miss Rosie Rottencrotch studied dramatics at San Jose State University, San Jose, Calif.*

J. Minor Wisdom*
    Judge
    (*New York Times*)

John Hodge Opera House Centennial
Gargling Oil Samuel J. Tilden
Ten Brook†
    Olcott, New York

John Senior, Junior
    New York City

JOHN WELLBORN WALLOP*
    University of California
    Berkeley, California

JOY BANG†
    Actress
    New York City

MR. JOYNT
    Marijuana Analyst
    Royal Canadian Mounted Police
    Crime Laboratory
    Alberta, Canada
    (*Christopher Logue*, True Stories. *London:
    A. P. Rushton, 1973.*)

JULY AUGUST SEPTEMBER
    (*Today's Health*)

Compare H. Wellborn Person.

†*Compare Joy Hooker, Superior, Wis. (sister of Gay Hooker).*

JUSTIN TUNE*
   Chorister
   Westminster Choir College (Class of 1947)
   Princeton, New Jersey

KATZ MEOW
   Hoquiam, Washington
   (*Collier's* magazine)

KATZ PAJAMA COMPANY†
   New York City

KRAPP PERFUMERY‡
   Marburg, West Germany

*Compare Melody Medley, Corpus Christi, Tex., and
Melody F. Sharp, children's choir director, Salem, Va.
(Associated Press).*

†*Compare Climax Underwear Co., Cincinnati, Oh.*

‡*The Compiler has a photograph of this establishment.*

74

Katz Meow, Hoquiam, Washington

KUHL BRIEZE
    Palm Harbor, Florida

LAKE TROUT*
    Attorney
    Los Angeles, California

LARRY DERRYBERRY†
    Attorney General
    Oklahoma City, Oklahoma

LAURA KNOTT TWINE
    Weaver‡
    Norwich, Connecticut

LAVENDER HANKEY§
    Los Angeles, California

*Brother of Brook Trout.

†Also Harry Derryberry, Lima, Oh., and Jerry Derryberry, Chattanooga, Tenn.

‡The Compiler has a photograph of this establishment.

§Compare Lacey Pantti, Republic, Mich.

Kuhl Brieze

Lavender Sidebottom*
    Masseuse, Elizabeth Arden
    New York City

Lawless & Lynch
    Attorneys
    Jamaica, New York

Lee Bum Suck†
    Foreign Minister
    Seoul, South Korea

*N.b.: Epitaph of Mr. Longbottom, who died young: Arse longa, vita brevis.

†Captain Robert E. Lee, U.S.N. (Ret.), noise monitor for the Montgomery County (Md.) Environmental Protection Department, changed his name to Roberto Edouardo Leon to qualify for "affirmative action" promotions ahead of his peers. "Finding loopholes is my job," he said. "This is an insult to Hispanics," fumed the governor's Commissioner on Hispanic Affairs.

LeGrunt E. Crapper*
    Johns Hopkins Hospital
    Baltimore, Maryland
    (Harvard Medical School *Alumni Bulletin*)

Le No Fuck Bébé
    French Rock Combo†
    (*Le Matin*)

Lesbia Lobo‡
    Golfer

Lettice Goedebed
    Johannesburg, South Africa

*His doctor reports that his name may subsequently have been changed to LeGrant.

†The Compiler has a photograph of this grouping.

‡Winner of the 1953 Broadmoor Ladies Invitational Golf Tournament in Colorado Springs, Colo.

LINUS KLUEMPER*
    Jasper, Indiana

LOBELIA RUGTWIT HILDEBIDDLE
    Psychology Student
    Occidental College
    Los Angeles, California

LOCH NESS HONTAS
    Tulane University Medical School
    New Orleans, Louisiana

LO FAT
    Retired Merchant Seaman
    New York City

*Attained celebrity in August 1955, when a fan in his
bedroom window wriggled five feet toward him and chopped
off the big toe of his right foot.

LOUIS GEORGE MAURICE ADOLPH ROCH
ALBERT ABEL ANTONIO ALEXANDRE NOÉ
JEAN LUCIEN DANIEL EUGÈNE JOSEPH-
LE-BRUN JOSEPHE-BARÊME THOMAS
THOMAS THOMAS THOMAS PIERRE
ARBON PIERRE-MAUREL BARTHELEMI
ARTUS ALPHONSE BERTRANI DIEUDONNÉ
EMANUEL JOSUÉ VINCENT LUC MICHEL
JULES-DE-LA-PLANE JULES-BAZIN JULIO
CESAR JULLIEN*
     Orchestra Conductor
     Sisteron, France

*Born in 1812 and named for members of his father's
orchestra, the Maestro was for obvious reasons known simply
as The Conductor Jullien. On June 15, 1854, he
presented "The Fireman's Quadrille" in the Crystal Palace
in New York. At the climax, by prearrangement, flames
burst out, engine bells rang in the streets, the windows were
broken, and firemen burst in, spewing water from their
hoses. Dozens of spectators collapsed as the crowd fought to
leave the hall. Jullien died, insane, in 1856.

Lovey Nookey Good*
   Texas State Health Department
   Austin, Texas

Loyal Lodge No. 296 Knights Of
Pythias Ponca City Oklahoma
Smith†
   Ponca City, Oklahoma

Luscious Pea‡
   The Charity Hospital
   New Orleans, Louisiana

Lynda Whynot§
   Wanton
   Providence, Rhode Island

*Compare Cassandra Nookiesnatch (possibly of Eskimo origin).

†Born August 21, 1876. Mencken, op. cit.

‡Compare Luscious Easter, Euclid, Oh., one of the first blacks to play for the Cleveland Indians.

§Convicted of lewd and wanton behavior in the Gemini Hotel (Providence Journal).

Lyulph Ydwallo Odin Nestor Egbert
Lyonel Toedmag Hugh Erchenwyne
Saxon Esa Cromwell Orma Nevill
Dysart Plantagenet Tollemache-
Tollemache
 Bentleigh, Otumoetai,
 Tauranga, New Zealand
 (*Burke's Peerage and Baronetage*)

Macgregor Suzuki
 Montreal, Canada

Madonna Ghostly
 Teacher
 Washington, D.C.

Magdalena Babblejack
 (*Maclean's* magazine)

Mrs. Maginis Oyster
 Social Leader
 San Rafael, California
 (*Social Register*)

MacGregor Suzuki

MAJOR QUAINTANCE*
    U.S. Army
    (*The New Yorker*)

MANLESS LAWRENCE†
    Virginia
    (Division of Vital Records and Health
    Statistics, Department of Health,
    Richmond, Virginia)

MARK CLARK VAN ARK
    Toledo, Ohio

MARMALADE P. VESTIBULE
    Door-to-door Firewood Salesman
    Cambridge, Massachusetts

Compare Major Minor, also U.S. Army.

†*Illegitimate. Compare Wedless Souvenir Campbell*
(Florida Bureau of Vital Statistics).

Mary Louise Pantzaroff*
   Huron County, Ohio

Mausoleum Jackson
      Virginia
      (Division of Vital Records and Health
      Statistics, Department of Health,
      Richmond, Virginia)

Melissy Dalciny Caldony Yankee
Pankee Devil-Take-The-Irishman
Garrison
      Boardinghouse Proprietress
      Tryon City, North Carolina

Membrane Pickle
      Virginia
      (Division of Vital Records and Health
      Statistics, Department of Health,
      Richmond, Virginia)

(Miss) Memory Lane
      Roslyn High School
      Roslyn, New York

*Compare Mary Maloof Teabaggy, Boston, Mass.

Mary Maloof Teabaggy, Boston

MEMORY LEAKE
   Contractor
   Tupelo, Mississippi

MENE MENE TEKEL UPHARSIN POND
   Hartford, Connecticut

MERCY BUMPUS*
   Wife of "General Tom Thumb"
   (both midgets)

(MISS) MIGNON HAMBURGER
   University of Wisconsin
   Madison, Wisconsin

MING-TOY EPSTEIN†
   New York City

MINNIE MAGAZINE‡
   Editor, *Time* magazine
   New York City

*Enjoyed the specialized distinction of being fought over by
the General and his tiny rival, Commodore Nutt.

†Long questioned by the Compiler, Ming-Toy's authenticity
has been established by S. J. Perelman and others.

‡Known to the complier.

Minnie Magazine, Magazine Editor

Moo, Boo, Goo, and Little Miss May
    New Orleans, Louisiana

Moon Unit and Dweezle Zappa*
    Hollywood, California

Muffy Virgin
    University of Chattanooga, Tennessee

Mustafa Kunt†
    Turkish Military Attaché
    Moscow, U.S.S.R.

My Struggle Driving School‡
    Johannesburg, South Africa

---

*Children of rock singer Frank Zappa.

†Occasion of much ribald official cable traffic, along with his vis-à-vis, Major R. Rectanus, U.S. Assistant Military Attaché, Moscow. Of Gen. Plastiras (Greece) Winston Churchill expressed the hope that he did not have "feet of clay."

‡Inspected, but not patronized, by the Compiler. Compare Fuzzle-Rub Motor Training School, Calcutta.

NAPOLEON B. BAREFOOT*
    Judge
    Wayne Co. Superior Court
    Goldsboro, N.C.

NEEDA CLIMAX
    Methodist Church Officer
    Centerville, Louisiana

NEVER FAIL†
    Louisville, Kentucky

NEWTON HOOTON
    Cambridge, Massachusetts

*Compare Judge Barefoot Sanders, U.S. District Court, Dallas, Tex.

†Mrs. Never Fail, exasperated by her husband's accounts of his achievements with "beautiful blondes," finally sought divorce (United Press). Compare Never Fail, Jr., builder, Tulsa, Okla. (known to the Compiler).

N. GUPPY*
    The Pond, Haddenham,
    Cambridgeshire, England

NITA BATH
    (*Philadelphia Evening Bulletin*)

NOBLE TEAT†
    Still Pond, Maryland

NOEL T. TWEET
    (*Business Week*)

NOSMO KING‡
    Pikesville, Maryland

Known to the Compiler. The fish is named for the family, not vice versa. In 1978 Barrister Michael Fysh defended a fishing rights case in the House of Lords before Lord Salmon.

†*Compare Faithful Teate, Dublin, "who wrote a quaint poem on the Trinity"* (Encyclopedia Britannica). *Also Noble Puffer, Superintendent of Schools, Cook County, Ill.; Noble Tickle, Rating, Royal Navy; Noble Butt, Boston; Noble Dick, Chairman, Dick Corporation, Pittsburgh, Pa.*

‡*Named for sign in waiting room of Dr. Brull, Sugarcane Road, Pikesville.*

Novice Fawcett
    President, Ohio State University
    Columbus, Ohio

Noway Near White*
    Shoe Salesman
    Columbus, Ohio

Odile, Odelia, Olive, Oliver,
Olivia, Ophelia, Odelin, Octave,
Octavia, Ovide, Onesia, Olite, Otto,
Ormes, and Opta Maynard†
    Abbeville, Louisiana

Odious Champagne‡
    Paper Mill Employee
    Winslow, Maine

*Compare January Snow White, Tampa, Fla.

†Dunkling, op. cit. Compare Assumpta, Attracta, Concepta, Redempta, and Rejoyca Custigan, of Ballybunion, Ireland, who won a traditional dance competition "because of their intricate footwork and they did not kick too high."

‡Compare Romeo Q. Champagne, state official, N.H.

O. Hell*
    Contractor
    Alto Adige, Italy

Sir Olateru Oba Alaiyeluwa
Olegbegi II
    The Olowo of Owo †

Oldmouse Waltz
    Federal Writers Project
    New Orleans, Louisiana

Oofty Goofty Bowman‡
    Shakespearean Actor
    Racine, Wisconsin
    (Milwaukee *Sentinel*)

Known to the Compiler.

†*"Son of Oba Alaiyeluwa Olabegi I; married, many sons and daughters; Educated, Owo Government School; Treasury Clerk in Owo Native Administration; Address, P.O. Box 1, Afin Oba Olowo, Owo; Telephone number: Owo 1"* (Who's Who).

‡*Named after a Ringling Bros. clown.*

OPHELIA TITTEY*
    Fall River, Massachusetts

FATHER O'PRAY†
    Church of St. Ignatius Loyola
    New York City

ORAL BLOW‡
    Portsmouth, Virginia
    (Bureau of Vital Statistics, State Board
    of Health, Richmond, Virginia)

*Compare Ophelia Bumps (reported by hospital where she was a patient), Ophelia Legg, Norwalk, Oh., and Ophelia Butts, Chattanooga, Tenn.

†Compare Rev. Goodness, Church of the Ascension, New York City (known to the Compiler), Rev. Hosanna, Denver, Colo., and Rev. God of Congaree, S.C.

‡Birth certificate examined by the Compiler. Compare fellow Virginian Easy Blow (who changed her name to Esther) and Oral Love, nursing home proprietor, Portland, Oreg.

Original Bug, Liverpool

ORANGE MARMALADE LEMON
    Wichita, Kansas

ORIGINAL BUG*
    Liverpool, England
    (*Liverpool Echo*)

OSBORN OUTHOUSE†
    Boston, Massachusetts

*Compare Septimus Bugg (*London* News Chronicle). *A Mr. Bugbee put himself on the entomological map by donating 30,000 parasitic wasps to the Smithsonian Institution* (Washington Post).

†*Compare A. Purdey Outhouse, perennial upper New York State office seeker.*

OSCAR ASPARAGUS*
     Basketball Star
     (*Maclean's* magazine)

PAFIA PIFIA PEFIA POFIA PUFIA DA COSTA
     Brazil
     (*Financial Times*)

DR. PARADISE GARDEN†
     Ear Surgeon
     Toronto, Ontario

PEARL HARBOR
     Telephone Operator of the *Birmingham News*
     Birmingham, Alabama

PENINNAH SWINGLE HOGENCAMP
UMBACH
     Spiritualist Minister
     Charleston, South Carolina

*Compare Baskerville Holmes, basketball player, Memphis
State University, Memphis, Tenn.

†Changed his name to Dr. Eden.

Oscar Asparagus, Basketball star

Dr. Penis*
> Plastic Surgeon
> San Francisco, California

Miss Pensive Cocke†
> Secretary
> U.S. Army Air Corps

*In a syndicated October 1980 New York Times article Dr. Penis advises women to have their breasts removed before signs of cancer appear. "We can't afford to wait for cancers to be detected, because by that time they're likely to have spread," he states.

†Compare Mrs. Seeman Glasscock; J. Badcock, Editor, London; B. Grocock, Teacher, Washington, D.C.; and D. Grewcock, Stockbroker, N.Y. The Koch Erecting Company is a major supplier to New York City. Cinderella Hardcock studied with the Art Instruction School, Minneapolis, Minn. Respectful attention is bestowed on the good Cornish family of Trebilcock and concerned awareness on Prof. A. O. J. Cockshut. W. J. Uglow Woolcock appears in Boyle's Court Guide for 1915. Cf. P. H. Reaney, The Origin of English Surnames. London: Routledge and Kegan Paul, 1967, pp. 209 et seq.

PETER BETER*
    Attorney
    Washington, D.C.

PHILI B. DEBOO†
    Professor of Geology
    Memphis, Tennessee

PHILOMENA CUNEGUNDE WEWE‡
    Hawaii

(MISS) PINK GASH§
    Hendersonville, North Carolina
    (*The Saturday Review*)

PLATO FOUFAS
    Real Estate
    Chicago, Illinois

PLUMMER & LEEK
    Plumbers
    Sheringham, Norfolk, England
    (London *Times*)

POSITIVE WASSERMANN JOHNSON*
    Evanston, Illinois

POTHUVILAGE BABYHAMY†
    U.S.A.

PRESERVED FISH, JR.‡
    New Bedford, Massachusetts

*"*Probably represents the indelicate humor of a medical
student.*"—H. L. Mencken*, The American Language.
New York: Alfred A. Knopf, 1936.

†*Changed her name in April 1974 to Ramya Briget
Pothuvilage. A. Przybysz of Detroit, Mich., changed his
name in 1940 to C. Przybysz* (Newsweek). *Ivan
Karamanov changed his name to John Dinkof Doikof*
(Maclean's *magazine*).

‡*Born in 1766; partner in firm said to market whale oil in
two grades: "good and bad." His father and other forebears
bore the same name. "There is no foundation to the oft
repeated story that his name was bestowed by a New Bedford
fisherman who found him as an infant adrift at sea in an
open boat"* (Dictionary of American Biography).

Preserved Fish, Jr.

Primrose Goo*
    Hawaii

(Miss) Ptarmigan Teale†
    Boston, Massachusetts

Quo Vadis Harris
    Medical Research Assistant
    Cambridge, Massachusetts
    (*New England Journal of Medicine*)

Raper Yowler
    Dayton, Ohio

Rapid Integration
    (*Newsweek*)

Rebecca Hammering Bang
    (*British Library/National Union Catalogue*)

*Compare Goo Gee Lo, Sydney, Australia, father of Fook
Hing, Fook Sing, Fook Ling, and Fook You (Sydney
Morning Herald).

†*Daughter of E. W. Teale, naturalist. Compare (Mrs.)
Birdie Peacock, Goldsboro, N.C.*

Rick O'Shea*
    Student
    Harrisburg, Oregon

Roman Pretzel†
    Tel Aviv, Israel

Ronald Supena‡
    Lawyer
    (*Philadelphia Evening Bulletin*)

Roosevelt Cabbagestalk§
    Pittsburgh, Pennsylvania
    (*Philadelphia Inquirer*, quoting *Advertising Age*)

Rosebud Rosenbloom
    Ethical Culture School
    New York City

Wounded by a demented sniper at Autzen Stadium, Eugene, Oreg.

†*A frequent correspondent in the* Jerusalem Post.

‡*S. Lawyer practices in Key Largo, Fla.*

§*Compare Zeditha Cabbagestalk, Safeway cashier, Washington, D.C.*

Rosetta Stone
    New York City

Rosey Vice*
    Multiple Larcenist
    Great Glemham, Suffolk, England

Rosy Yass†
    Cincinnati, Ohio

Dr. Safety First‡
    Tulsa, Oklahoma

Salome Casanova§
    Havana, Cuba, and Madrid, Spain

*Possessed of a notable "green thumb," she was released from confinement each spring to assist in planting.

†So taken with her maiden name that after marriage she maintained a separate telephone directory listing for it. Compare Rosie Rump, Bettendorf, Ia., Rosie Rump, San Francisco, Calif., and Barbara Fatt Heine, New York City (New York Times).

‡Another Safety First is in his nineties in Seal Beach, Calif.

§Known to the Compiler.

SANDWITH DRINKER
    University of Pennsylvania (Class of 1971)
    Philadelphia, Pennsylvania

SANTIAGO NUDELMAN
    Publisher
    Brazil

SARA STRUGGLES NICELY
    Clearwater, Florida
    (*Cleveland Plain Dealer*)

MRS. SCREECH*
    Singing Teacher
    Victoria, British Columbia

SERIOUS MISCONDUCT†
    Welwyn, England

**Wife of Dr. Screech, Dentist.*
†*Compare General Error, Pueblo, Colo.*

LT. GEN. HIS HIGHNESS SHRI SHRI SHRI
SHRI SHRI SHRI SHRI SHRI SHRI SHRI
SHRI SHRI SHRI SHRI SHRI SHRI SHRI
SHRI SHRI SHRI SHRI SHRI SHRI SHRI
SHRI SHRI SHRI SHRI SHRI SHRI SHRI
SHRI SHRI SHRI SHRI SHRI SHRI SHRI
SHRI SHRI SHRI SHRI SHRI SHRI SHRI
SHRI SHRI SHRI SHRI SHRI SHRI SHRI
SHRI SHRI SHRI SHRI SHRI SHRI SHRI
SHRI SHRI SHRI SHRI SHRI SHRI SHRI
SHRI SHRI SHRI SHRI SHRI SHRI SHRI
SHRI SHRI SHRI SHRI SHRI SHRI SHRI
SHRI SHRI SHRI SHRI SHRI SHRI SHRI
SHRI SHRI SHRI SHRI SHRI SHRI SHRI
SHRI SHRI SHRI SHRI SHRI SHRI SHRI
SHRI SHRI SHRI SHRI SHRI SHRI SHRI
MAHARAJADHIRAJ RAJ RAJESHWAR SHRI
MAHARJA-I-RAJGAN MARARAJA SIR
YADVINDRA SINGH MAHENDRA BAHADUR,
YADU VANSHAVATANS BHATTI KUL
BHUSHAN RAJPRAMUKH OF PATIALA*
India and London, England

*Born in 1913, the Maharaja of Patiala is also the leader
of the Sikh community, all of whose members bear the
surname Singh (meaning lion). The sequence in the first
part of the title is usually contracted to "Shri 108."

Lt. Gen. H.H. Shri Shri Shri (etc... 108 times) Maharajadhiraj, the Maharaja of Patiala

SHAKEY T. MUDBONE
   Hudson, New York

SHANDA LEAR*
   Battle Creek, Michigan

SHINE SOON SUN†
   Geophysicist
   Houston, Texas

SHLOMO TURTLEDOVE
   Tel Aviv, Israel

SIDDHARTHA GREENBLATT
   (*Harper's* magazine)

Of the Lear Jet Lears.

†*Compare Moon Bong Kang, Korean Ambassador to
Switzerland, and Dong-Dong Kong, piano student,
Juilliard School of Music, New York City.*

SILENCE BELLOWS*
    Editor, *Christian Science Monitor*

COMMANDER SINK, U.S.N.
    Fort Washington, Maryland

SODAWATER BOTTLEWALLA†
    Bombay, India
    (*New York Times*)

SOLOMON GEMORAH
    Brooklyn, New York

DR. STARK STARING
    Professor, University of Utrecht
    Holland
    (*Sunday Telegraph*)

STRANGEWAYS PIGG STRANGEWAYS
    Cricket Star
    London, England

Vermont Connecticut Royster was editor of the other reliable American paper, the Wall Street Journal.

†*Walla is a Parsee suffix indicating occupation, comparable to the* "er" *in Baker.*

Tarantula Turner, Schoolgirl

SUBMIT CLAPP*
Easthampton, Massachusetts

(MISS) SUE YU
Library Card Holder
Flushing, New York

SUPARPORN POOPATTANA
New York City

MRS. TACKABERRY McADOO†
Social Leader
New York City
(*Social Register*)

TARANTULA TURNER
New Orleans, Louisiana

*Distant kinswoman of the Compiler. Married Asabel Clark
(1737–1822). Mother of Eliakim, Eleasar, Submit, Asakel,
Bohan (died in infancy), Bohan (the second), Electa, Jerusha,
Achsah, Lucas, and Jared. Compare Supply Clapp Thwing,
Harvard class of 1837.*

†*Known to the Compiler.*

Taura Loura Goldfarb
New York City

Tetley Ironside Tetley Jones
Chairman, Tetley Tea Company
London, England

T. Fud Pucker Tucker
Bountiful, Utah

T. Guempel Glomp
(Allentown, Pennsylvania, *Morning Call*)

Theanderblast Mischgedeigle Sump*
Insurance Agent
Orillia, Ontario

T. Hee
Restaurant Employee
New York City

Insists on the inclusion of his middle name.

THEODOLPHUS J. POONTANG
   Oakland, California
   (*San Francisco Examiner*)

MRS. THERESA PICNICK*
   Nutritionist
   Worcester, Massachusetts

THOMAS CRAPPER†
   Inventor of Flush Toilet
   London, England

Compare Bacon Chow, nutritionist, Johns Hopkins School of Public Health, Baltimore, Md., and Lo Fat, cook aboard S.S. President Wilson.

†*His biography is aptly titled* Flushed With Pride. *Compare Toilet Jacobs, E. C. Crapp, Washington, D.C., and Gladstone P. Lillycrap, U.S. Attorney. Lotta Crap is the daughter of Paul Crap of the Crap Bakery, Greencastle, Ind. Dr. Sylvan Stool is a prominent Philadelphia surgeon.*

Mrs T. Picnick, Nutritionist

THUSNELDA NEUSBICKLE
   Wellesley College
   Wellesley, Massachusetts

MRS. TINY SPRINKLE*
   New York City

TOPPIE SMELLIE
   TV Chicken Coating Mix Endorser

TRAILING ARBUTUS VINES†
   Cumberland Mountains, Tennessee

*Compare A. Tiny Hurt, Portland, Oreg., and Judith Moist.
†Mencken, op. cit.

Ufuk Restaurant*
    Izmir, Turkey

Ulysses Tyrebiter
    Boston, Massachusetts

Unable To Fornicate†
    Indian Chief
    Northwestern U.S.

Urban Shocker‡
    Pitcher, New York Yankees
    New York City

Ure A. Pigg
    Restaurateur
    Portland, Oregon
    (*Oregon Journal*)

*Patronized by the Compiler.

†Reported by Mencken. Compare Shun Fornication, Barebones,
N.H. Fly-Fornication was a good Puritan name, given to
children born out of wedlock.

‡Compare Fair Hooker, end, Cleveland Browns.

Ufuk Restaurant, Izmir, Turkey

URINE MCZEAL*
   Washington County, Florida

URSULA WOOP
   National Typewriting Champion
   East Germany

U.S. BOND†
   Safe Deposit Manager
   Harvard Trust Company
   Cambridge, Massachusetts

VASELINE LOVE‡
   Jackson, Tennessee

*Compare Argo Pisson, Quality Control Engineer,
Raytheon Corporation, Lexington, Mass.; and Kitty Peed,
Cape Coral, Fla., who died in a light-airplane accident.

†Compare U.S. Flag, Kansas, Oh., whose name ("not
initials") was suggested to his mother by a passing peddler
(Toledo Blade).

‡Compare Vaseline Maleria. Also Radical Love, Selective
Service registrant, Washington, D.C., Love Kisses Love,
Mess Attendant, U.S.S. Lexington, and Love Newlove,
Toronto, Ont. Natania Shitlove changed her name to
Laura Shitlove.

Veniamin Dymshits
    Chairman, Gosplan
    U.S.S.R.

Mr. Venus Bonaparte
    (London *Times*)

Verbal Funderburk*
    Lakeland, Florida

Professor Verbal Snook
    Chairman, Mathematics Department
    Oral Roberts University
    Tulsa, Oklahoma

Mr. Vice†
    Malefactor
    New Orleans, Louisiana

Mrs. Funderburk wrote to a collaborator of the Compiler to ask if she had the funniest name in the world. Her anxieties were laid to rest.

†*Arrested 820 times and convicted 421, probably a record* (International Herald Tribune).

Vile Albert

VILE ALBERT
    St. Johnsbury, Vermont

VIOLET ORGAN*
    Art Historian
    New York City

VIRGINIA MAY SWEATT STRONG
    Memphis, Tennessee

VOID NULL†
    Schoolteacher
    San Diego, California

VOLUME DINGLE‡
    Tampa, Florida

*Biographer of the American painter Robert Henri. She never married. Compare Violet Butt, Washington, D.C.

†Born January 3, 1904, in Mexico, Mo., to Henrietta and Thomas Jefferson Null, whose occupation is enigmatically given as "panatorium." Compare Romeo Zero, New York City.

‡His wife threw out his pants, containing his life's savings (Tampa Tribune). Compare Elisha Peanut Tingle, Gumboro, Del.

Mr. Vroom
>Motorcycle Dealer
>Port Elizabeth, South Africa
>(*New York Times*)

Wambly Bald
>Reporter, *New York Post*
>New York City

Warren Peace
>Williams College, Massachusetts

Sir W. C. Dampier-Whetham
>Upwater Lodge, Cambridge, England

Welcome Baby Darling
>Advertising Man
>Greenwich, Connecticut

William McKinley Louisiana
Leveebust Smith
>Richmond, Virginia

Wun Tu O'Clock
>Boston, Massachusetts

Mr Vroom, Motorcycle Dealer, Port Elizabeth, South Africa

WYRE & TAPPING*
   Detectives
   New York City

YELBERTON ABRAHAM TITTLE
   Quarterback, New York Giants
   New York City

ZEPPELIN W. WONG†
   Attorney
   San Francisco, California

ZEZOZOSE ZADFRACK‡
   California

ZILPHER SPITTLE
   English parish record
   (*Maclean's* magazine)

Zip A-Dee-Doo Daub*
   La Luz, New Mexico
   (*The Miami Herald*)

Dr. Zoltan Ovary†
   Gynecologist, New York Hospital
   New York City

Zowie Bowie‡
   England

Firstborn son of Mr. & Mrs. Daub, who waited 12 years to have a baby, and stated that the name "just seemed right."

†*And, of course, Madame Ovary.*

‡*Son of rock singer David Bowie.*

Void Null

INDEX

Aass, 11
Adams, 13
Agony, 35
Albert, 123
Angeledes, 20
*Apostle, 27*n
Argue, 11
Asparagus, 98
Babblejack, 83
Babyhamy, 102
*Badcock, 100*n
Bagge of Boo, 52
Bald, 124
Ball, 25, 29
Balls, 56
Banana, 22
*Banfill, 66*n
Bang, 73, 104
*Banks, 27*n
Barebones, 67
Barefoot, 91
Bath, 92
Bedient, 24
*Belcher, 16*n
*Bellie, 31*n
Bellows, 111
Belsky, 14
Berman, 61
Beter, 101
Bidet, 22
*Biggerdick, 32*n
Blitch, 70
Blob, 25

Blow, 95
Boeras, 18
Bonaparte, 121
Bond, 70, 120
*Bonebrake, 18, 40*n
*Bonecutter, 41*n
*Bones, 57*n
*Bonesetter, 41*n
*Boobert, 59*n
*Boozer, 31*n
Boring, 19
Bottlewalla, 111
Bottom, 35
*Bottoms, 35*n
Bowie, 129
Bowman, 94
Breckenridge, 37
Bridge, 16
Brieze, 76
*Broadmoor, 79*n
Broccoli, 16
Brothers, 28
Bug, 97
*Bugbee, 97*n
*Bugg, 69*n, 97*n
Bull, 19, 20
*Bumps, 95*n
Bumpus, 88
Burger, 51
Burp, 16
Burst, 61
*Butcher, 41*n

*Butt, 35*n, 92*n, 123*n
*Butts, 95*n
Buzzard, 18
*Cabangbang, 14*n
Cabbagestalk, 105
*Campbell, 85*n
Carr, 61
*Carver, 41*n
Casanova, 54, 106
Champagne, 6, 93
*Cheatem, 27*n
Cheatham, 27
Cheatum, 27
Cherry, 14
*Chow, 115*n
Church, 27
Clapp, 29, 113
Clapsaddle, 29
*Clark, 113*n
*Climax, 74*n, 91*
Clutch, 65
Clutter, 6, 45
Cock, 32
Cocke, 100
*Cockshut, 100*n
Cohen, 54
*Collision, 54*n
*Conception, 62*n
*Copp, 25*n
Cox, 58, 66
*Crap, 115*n

*Crapp, 115*n
Crapper, 79, 115
*Creep, vi, 57*n
*Cretin, 19*n
Crook, 25
*Crooke, 25*n
Cumming, 38
*Custigan, 93*n
*Cutter, 41*n
da Costa, 98
Dalley, 42
Dampier-Whetham, 126
Dangle, 67
Darling, 124
Da Silva, 22
Daub, 127
*Day, 28*n
Deadman, 38
Deboo, 101
de Jesus, 35
de Horsey, 65
*Dement, 42*n
Dente, 10
Derryberry, 76
*Dicebat, 51*n
*Dick, 32, 92*n
Digger, 57
Dingle, 123
*Ditty, 66*n
Doctor, 41
*Doikof, 102*n
*Dollar, 41*n

Dong-Dong Kong, 108n
Doolittle, 42
Dotti, 42
Drinker, 107
Dubbs, 22
Dukes, 101n
Dummer, 19n
Dymshits, 121
Easter, 82n
Eden, 98n
Elbow, 41
Epstein, 88
Error, 107n
Eubanks, 44
Everybodytalksabout, 25
Fail, 91
Falces, 41n
Fang, 45
Fangboner, 6-7, 66
Fast, 70n
Fat, 80, 115n
Fawcett, 93
Fealey, 47
Filler, 45n
Finger, 47n
Finkelstein, 16, 69
First, 106
Fish, 48n, 102
Flag, 120
Folts, 38
Fong, 61
Fook, 104n

Ford, 61
Foufas, 101
Frett, 25n
Frilli, 70
Frost, 67n
Fuchs, 62
Funderburk, 121
Futch, 66n
Fuzzey, 52
Fuzzle-Rub, 90n
Fysh, 92n
Garage, 61
Garden, 98
Gargle, 45n
Garrison, 86
Gash, 101
Gass, 44n
Gemorah, 111
Gesundheit, 70
Ghostly, 83
Glasscock, 56, 100n
Glomp, 114
Gluck, 59
God, 27n, 95n
Goedebed, 79
Goldfarb, 113
Goo, 104
Good, 82
Goodness, 95n
Goo Gee Lo, 104n
Gooing, 38
Goon, 42
Greenblatt, 111
Greene, 47
Grewcock, 100n

Griesedick, 32n
Grocock, 100n
Grossnickel, 14n
Grubb, 71
Gryp, 48
Guppy, 92
Habakkuk, 65
Hamburger, 88
Hamlin, 13n
Hankey, 76
Harbor, 98
Hardcock, 100n
Hare, 59
Harison, 56
Harris, 72n, 104
Hassenpflug, 66n
Headline, 59
Hee, 114
Heimerdinger, 35n
Heine, 106n
Heinrich, 61
Hell, 94
Hildebiddle, 6, 80
Hoar, 67n
Hogg, 69
Holmes, 98
Hontas, 80
Hooker, 73n, 118n
Hooton, 91
Horsey, 65n
Hosanna, 27n, 95n
Human, 57n
Hunnybun, 47

Hurt, 117n
Hymen, 66
Icenoggle, 67n
Integration, 104
Jackson, 11, 86
Jacobs, 115n
Jejeebhoy, 71
Jockitch, 71
Johnson, 7, 102
Jones, 32n, 48, 114
Joynt, 73
Judge, 72n
Jullien, 81
Karamanov, 102n
Katz, 74
Keel, 44
Kilgore, 48n
King, 92
Kluemper, 80
Koch, 100
Krapp, 74
Kunt, 90
Kutylpov, 22n
Lane, 86
Lawless, 78
Lawrence, 85
Leake, 88
Lear, 108
Lee, 78n
Lee Bum Suck, 78
Leek, 102
Legg, 95n
Lemon, 97
Ley, 52
Lillycrap, 115n

Lobo, 79
Longbottom, 78n
Love, 20, 95n, 120
Lurch, 52
Lynch, 78
McAdoo, 113
Macaroni, 16n
Macaulay, 10
McBean, 10n
McZeal, 120
Magazine, 88
Maleria, 120n
Marsh, 44
May, 90
Maynard, 93
Medley, 74n
Meow, 7, 74
Metalious, 51n
Miccolo, 66
Million, 45
Miner, 13
Minor, 37, 85n
Misconduct, 107
Moist, 117n
Mole, 57n
Moon Bong Kang, 108n
Moron, 11
Mouser, 19n
Mpofu, 54
Mudbone, 107
Mutual, 54n
Neusbickle, 117
Newlove, 120n
Nicely, 107

No Fuck Bébé, Le, 79
Nookiesnatch, 82n
Nudelman, 107
Null, 123
Obedience, 24
O'Clock, 124
Odor, 71
Olegbegi, 94
O'Pray, 95
Organ, 29, 123
O'Shea, 105
Outhouse, 97
Ovary, 127
Overcash, 48n
Oyster, 83
Paine, 41n
Pancake, 27
Pantti, 76n
Pantzaroff, 86
Parts, 14n
Passwater, 70n
Paternite, 47n
Patiala, 109
Payne, 41n
Pea, 82
Peace, 124
Peacock, 104n
Pecker, 24n
Peckeroff, 66n
Pecor, 24
Peed, 120n
Penis, 100
Person, 73n
Pettibone, 101n

Phibbs, 11
Pickle, 6, 86
Picnick, 115
Pigg, 118
Pine-Coffin, 44
Pinkypank, 37
Pisson, 120n
Pitt, 57n
Plant, 57n
Plastiras, 90n
Pleasure, 66n
Plick, 41
Plummer, 102
Plunkett-Ernle-Erle-Drax, 31n
Pond, 88
Poontang, 115
Poopattana, 113
Popcorn, 45
Posthumus, 57n
Pothuvilage, 102n
Pretzel, 105
Prick, 32
Przvbysz, 102n
Puffer, 92n
Pugh, 65
Pulls, 45n
Pusser, 19
Pussy, 51
Quaintance, 85
Quattlebaum, 10
Quick, 35n
Quick-Park, 57n
Rainwater, 51
Rash, 38
Rectanus, 90n

Repentigny, 51n
Restrepo, 24
Reuss, 61
Roll, 62
Romero, 42
Rosenbloom, 105
Rottencrotch, 71n
Royster, 111n
Rump, 106n
Salmon, 92n
Sanders, 91n
Schnauz, 47
Schreck-Purola, 67
Schumuk, 42
Schytt, 20
Screech, 40n, 45n, 107
Senior, 72
September, 73
Seraphim, 28
Sharp, 74n
Shine Soon Sun, 108
Shippe, 31n
Shitlove, 120n
Shitole, 10
Shittachitta, 10n
Shivers, 67
Shocker, 118
Shovel, 31
Shytti, 10n
Sidebottom, 78
Silver, 70
Sin, 22
Singh, 109

Sink, 111
Slappe, 67n
Smallpeice, 16
Smellie, 117
Smith, 14n, 19, 72n, 82, 126
Snook, 121
Snooze, 56
Snow, 67n
Snowball, 54
Somchittindepata, 10
Spector, 59
Spittle, 126
Sprinkle, 117
Staring, 111
Steele, 27
Step, 48
Stone, 106
Stool, 115n
Strangeways, 111
Strong, 123
Stubbs, 28
Sump, 114
Supena, 105
Suzuki, 83
Swallow, 35n
Swindella, 27n

Taione, 38
Tapping, 126
Tarte, 51
Teabaggy, 86n
Teale, 104
Teat, 92
Teate, 92n
Ten Brook, 72
Tetley, 114
Thigpen, 35
Thwing, 113
Tickle, 92n
Tingle, 123n
Tittey, 95
Tittle, 126
Tollemache, 83
Toodles, 41
Toot, 37
Toothaker, 45n
Toto, 58
Tottle, 13
Trebilcock, 100n
Trouble, 14
Trout, 76
Tucker, 114
Tune, 74
Turner, 113
Turtledove, 108

Twaddle, 62
Tweet, 92
Twine, 76
Tyrebiter, 118
Ufuk, 118
Umbach, 98
Unable to Fornicate, 7, 118
Uren, 70n
Van Ark, 85
Vereneseneckock-krockoff, 48
Vestibule, 85
Vice, 106, 123
Vines, 117
Virgin, 90
Von Garlic, 57
von Zitzewitz, 69
Vroom, 124
Wack, 16
Wallop, 73
Waltz, 6, 94
Warmflash, 44, 45n
Washington, 72n
Weewee, 101n
Weisenburg, 69n

Werbezirk-Piffl, 54
Wewe, 101
White, 18, 93
Whur, 36
Whynot, 82
Wierdo, 42n
Willfahrt, 47n
Wind, 47n
Wing On, 57n
Winneboso, 14
Wisdom, 72
Womble, 20
Woolcock, 100n
Woop, 120
Worm, 13
Wright, 27n
Wyre, 126
Yass, 106
Yoho, 6, 44
Yowler, 104
Yu, 113
Zadfrack, 126
Zamost, 69
Zappa, 90
Zerk, 10n
Zero, 123n
Zipper, 11